Looking at the Stars

Written by
Cath Jones

Eve the fox was a hot shot on the stars.

Steve the rabbit was not!

Eve called on Steve. Tap, tap, tap.

"Do you feel like looking at the stars with me?" asked Eve.

"What is a star?" asked Steve.

"A star is made up of hot gas," said Eve.

As the sun set, they set off together to hunt for a dark spot to look at the stars.

The best sites are on top of a hill or in a park, and not near street lights.

Come on, Steve! Winter is a good time to look up at the stars. It is dark a lot of the time.

Looking at stars can be like looking at a map. You can use them to navigate.

There are patterns in the stars too. Look, that pattern of seven stars is the big dipper.

And you might see the Pole Star too.

Look. That is the moon.

We see the same side of the moon all the time. As it orbits the planet, the moon turns.

So we never see the far side of the moon. For us, the far side is the dark side of the moon.